J 00074860
599.363 Bowman, Chris,
BOW Red squirrels

SCOTLAND COUNTY MEMORIAL LIBRARY
MEMPHIS, MO 63555

This project is supported by the Institute of Museum and Library Services under the provisions of the Library Services and Technology Act as administered by the Missouri State Library, a division of the Office of the Secretary of State.

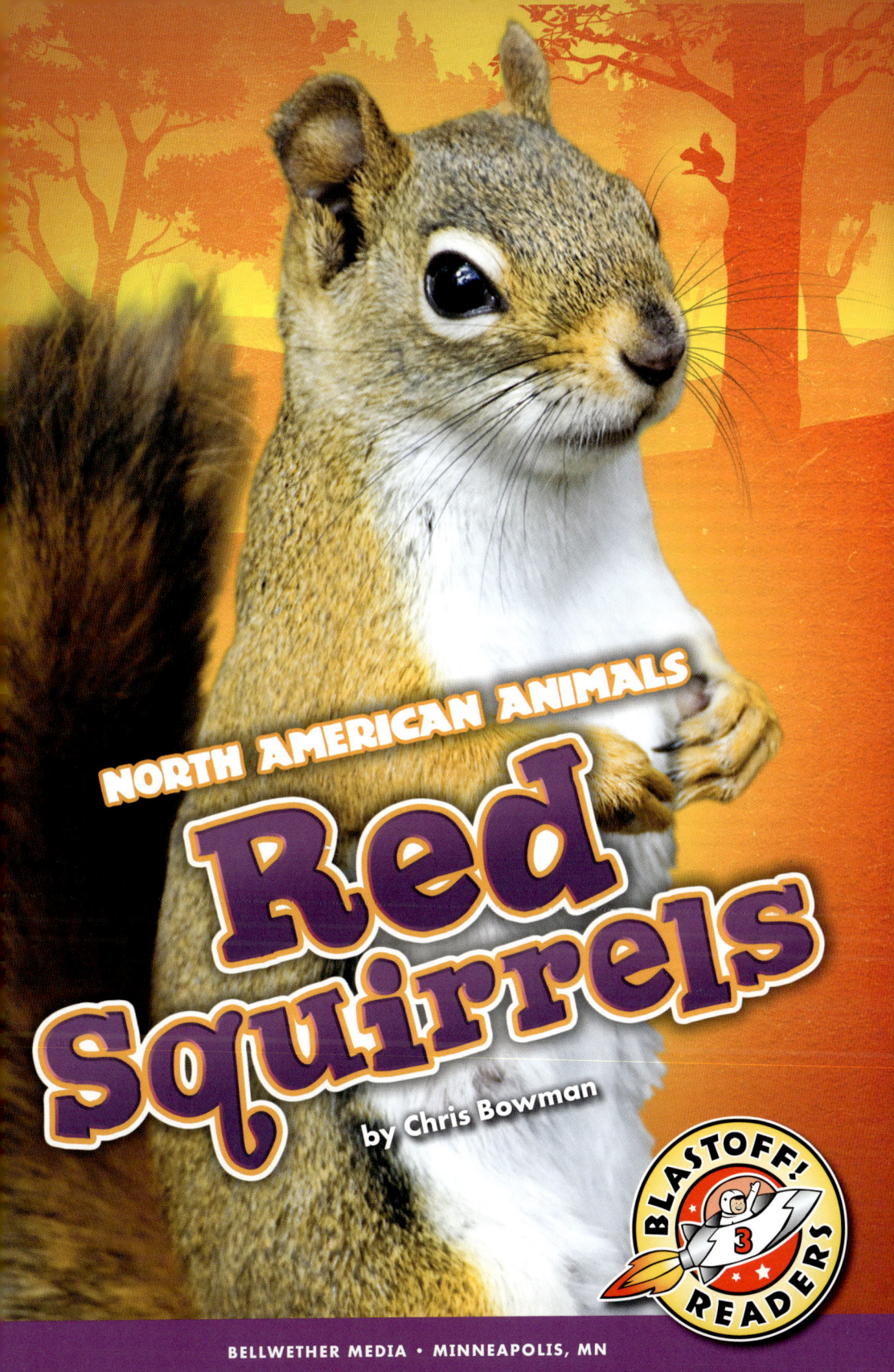

NORTH AMERICAN ANIMALS
Red Squirrels

by Chris Bowman

BLASTOFF! READERS 3

BELLWETHER MEDIA • MINNEAPOLIS, MN

Note to Librarians, Teachers, and Parents:

Blastoff! Readers are carefully developed by literacy experts and combine standards-based content with developmentally appropriate text.

Level 1 provides the most support through repetition of high-frequency words, light text, predictable sentence patterns, and strong visual support.

Level 2 offers early readers a bit more challenge through varied simple sentences, increased text load, and less repetition of high-frequency words.

Level 3 advances early-fluent readers toward fluency through increased text and concept load, less reliance on visuals, longer sentences, and more literary language.

Level 4 builds reading stamina by providing more text per page, increased use of punctuation, greater variation in sentence patterns, and increasingly challenging vocabulary.

Level 5 encourages children to move from "learning to read" to "reading to learn" by providing even more text, varied writing styles, and less familiar topics.

Whichever book is right for your reader, Blastoff! Readers are the perfect books to build confidence and encourage a love of reading that will last a lifetime!

This edition first published in 2016 by Bellwether Media, Inc.

No part of this publication may be reproduced in whole or in part without written permission of the publisher. For information regarding permission, write to Bellwether Media, Inc., Attention: Permissions Department, 5357 Penn Avenue South, Minneapolis, MN 55419.

Library of Congress Cataloging-in-Publication Data

Bowman, Chris, 1990- author.
  Red Squirrels / by Chris Bowman.
    pages cm. – (Blastoff! readers. North American Animals)
  Summary: "Simple text and full-color photography introduce beginning readers to red squirrels. Developed by literacy experts for students in kindergarten through third grade"– Provided by publisher.
  Audience: Ages 5-8.
  Audience: K to grade 3.
  Includes bibliographical references and index.
  ISBN 978-1-62617-336-1 (hardcover : alk. paper)
  1. Tamiasciurus–Juvenile literature. 2. Squirrels–Juvenile literature. [1. Red squirrels.] I. Title. II. Series: Blastoff! readers. 3, North American animals.
  QL737.R68B69 2016
  599.36'3–dc23
                              2015028682

Text copyright © 2016 by Bellwether Media, Inc. BLASTOFF! READERS and associated logos are trademarks and/or registered trademarks of Bellwether Media, Inc. SCHOLASTIC, CHILDREN'S PRESS, and associated logos are trademarks and/or registered trademarks of Scholastic Inc.

Printed in the United States of America, North Mankato, MN.

Table of Contents

What Are Red Squirrels?	4
Finding Food	12
Noisy Animals	16
Squirrel Kits	18
Glossary	22
To Learn More	23
Index	24

What Are Red Squirrels?

Red squirrels are small **rodents** found across Alaska and Canada.

These **mammals** also live in the Rocky Mountains and the northeastern United States.

Red squirrels have rusty-red backs and white bellies. White fur surrounds their eyes. During winter, some grow **ear tufts**.

Their **bushy** tails are thin for squirrels. Their curved claws and strong legs help them climb.

Red squirrels are smaller than many other squirrels. They weigh about 7 to 9 ounces (198 to 255 grams).

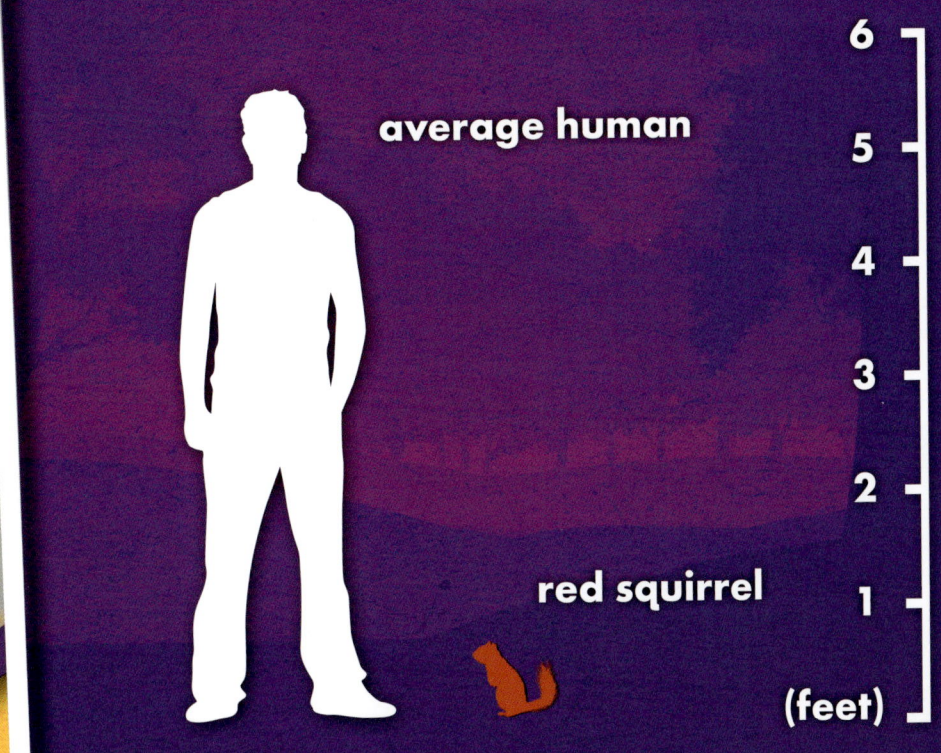

They grow to be about 10 to 15 inches (25 to 38 centimeters) long. Their tails measure about 4 to 6 inches (10 to 15 centimeters) of this length.

Red squirrels usually live in forests. They are most active during early mornings and evenings.

These squirrels build nests on branches and in tree holes. Some live in underground **burrows**.

Finding Food

Red squirrels are **omnivores**. They often eat seeds, nuts, and fruits.

On the Menu

green pine cones

maple seeds

raspberries

eastern bluebird eggs

morel mushrooms

acorns

They also eat insects, bird eggs, and mushrooms. Sometimes they lick up tree sap!

In the fall, the squirrels gather food for the winter. They store food in **middens** around their **territories**.

Middens are often under logs, by trees, or in the ground.

Noisy Animals

Red squirrels guard their middens. They give warning calls when an animal is too close. They stamp their feet and jerk their tails.

Animals to Avoid

American martens

coyotes

bald eagles

great gray owls

Cooper's hawks

Canada lynx

These squirrels also call when **predators** are near. Red squirrels avoid **raptors** like owls and hawks.

Squirrel Kits

Red squirrels give birth to **kits** in spring. Some females have a second litter in late summer. At first, the **newborns** stay in the nest.

Baby Facts

Names for babies: kits, kittens, or pups

Size of litter: 3 to 5 kits

Length of pregnancy: 31 to 35 days

Time spent with mom: 10 to 12 weeks

They explore outside the nest after about eight weeks.

Soon, the squirrels find their own territories. Time to gather food!

Glossary

burrows—holes or tunnels that some animals dig for homes

bushy—thick and fluffy

ear tufts—fur in the ears of red squirrels for warmth

kits—baby red squirrels

mammals—warm-blooded animals that have backbones and feed their young milk

middens—piles of food that rodents hide

newborns—babies that were just recently born

omnivores—animals that eat both plants and animals

predators—animals that hunt other animals for food

raptors—large birds that hunt other animals; raptors have excellent eyesight and powerful talons.

rodents—small animals that gnaw on their food

territories—the land areas where animals live

To Learn More

AT THE LIBRARY
Leaf, Christina. *Gray Squirrels*. Minneapolis, Minn.: Bellwether Media, 2015.

Rose, Nancy. *The Secret Life of Squirrels*. New York, N.Y.: Little, Brown and Company, 2014.

Schuh, Mari. *Squirrels*. North Mankato, Minn.: Capstone Press, 2015.

ON THE WEB
Learning more about red squirrels is as easy as 1, 2, 3.

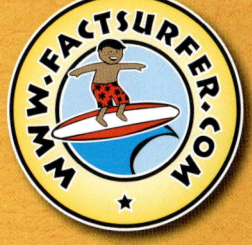

1. Go to www.factsurfer.com.

2. Enter "red squirrels" into the search box.

3. Click the "Surf" button and you will see a list of related web sites.

With factsurfer.com, finding more information is just a click away.

Index

Alaska, 4
burrows, 11
calls, 16, 17
Canada, 4
claws, 7
climb, 7
colors, 6, 7
ear tufts, 6
explore, 20
feet, 16
females, 18
food, 12, 13, 14, 21
forests, 10
fur, 6
gather, 14, 21
guard, 16
kits, 18, 19
legs, 7
mammals, 5
middens, 14, 15, 16

nests, 11, 18, 20
omnivores, 12
predators, 17
range, 4, 5
Rocky Mountains, 5
rodents, 4
seasons, 6, 14, 18
size, 8, 9
tails, 7, 9, 16
territories, 14, 21
United States, 5

The images in this book are reproduced through the courtesy of: BMJ, front cover, p. 7 (top left, center, bottom); Brian Lasenby, pp. 4, 8; Mircea Costina/ Alamy, pp. 6, 10; David P. Lewis, p. 7 (top right); Minden Pictures/ SuperStock, pp. 11, 15, 16, 18; Don Johnston/ age fotostock/ SuperStock, p. 12; Africa Studio, p. 13 (top left); SAJE, p. 13 (top right); gresei, p. 13 (center left); Bonnie Taylor Barry, p. 13 (center right); Taiftin, p. 13 (bottom left); Dionisvera, p. 13 (bottom right); Chris & Tilde Stuart/ FLPA, p. 14; Erni, p. 17 (top left, bottom right); Cynthia Kidwell, p. 17 (top right); FloridaStock, p. 17 (center left); rokopix, p. 17 (center right); Steve Byland, p. 17 (bottom left); KellyNelson, p. 19; Julie DeRoche/ Glow Images, p. 20; Allan Oman/ Glow Images, p. 21.

SCOTLAND COUNTY MEMORIAL LIBRARY
MEMPHIS, MO 63555